TENDING THE FIRE
The Ritual Men's Group

TENDING

THE FIRE

The Ritual Men's Group

Wayne Liebman

Copyright © 1991 Wayne Liebman

Published by   Ally Press
                524 Orleans Street
                St. Paul, MN 55107

Printed in The United States of America
by Thompson Shore, Inc.

ISBN 0-915408-45-7
Cover design and Lost Dog logo by Holly Hudson
Book design by Paul Feroe

91 92 93 94 95 5 4 3 2

Library of Congress Cataloging in Publication Data
Liebman, Wayne, 1948—
    Tending the fire : the ritual men's group / Wayne Liebman.
        p.   cm.
    ISBN 0-915408-45-7 : $7.00
    1. Men--Psychology. 2. Small groups. 3. Ritualization.
    4. Social Groups--Case studies. I. Title
    HQ1090.L54 1991
    302.3'4--dc20

ACKNOWLEDGMENTS

This book is for men who are, or want to be, in a small ritual men's group. The resurgence of this ancient form is an outgrowth of conferences for men inspired by the poet Robert Bly in the early 1980's and given momentum by Michael Meade, James Hillman and others. Although I draw on material from groups I've participated in, I don't intend this to be a manual or handbook. I'm writing to describe, as thoroughly as I can, the implications of small ritual groups, the issues, problems and possibilities inherent in them. I hope that a man reading this will gain a clearer sense of what he wants from a group, and what he needs to do to get it.

I've had help from many friends in writing this. Jane Alexander Stewart taught me what it is to take metaphor into action and I owe her more than I can say. Daniel Attias kept me on course throughout with his enthusiasm and thoughtful counsel. I'm thankful to Rick Matthews, Randy Scott, Eric Field, Mitchell May, Eric Wright, Jim Gordezky, David Langer, Bruce Wallenstein, John Densmore and John Alexis Viereck for their careful reading of the manuscript, and to Carole Burstein for her insight into myth. Paul Feroe has been a consistently supportive and discriminating editor.

My conviction about the importance of small ritual groups to men stems directly from my own involvement in a group. For their courage in wandering through uncharted lands, I want to express my gratitude and admiration to all the members of Lost Dog Men's Council, past and present.

—W.L.

CONTENTS

INTRODUCTION

ONE
  LOOKING FOR IRON JOHN 3
    The Nature of the Ritual Group
    Mythological Reality and the Container
      of the Ritual Group

TWO
  INVITING THE MYTHOLOGICAL 13
    Working Mythologically
    The Talking Stick
    Responding to Myths, Fairy Stories, Dreams
      and Personal Dramas
    Creating Rituals
    Feelings and Resistance to Feelings
    Turning Up the Heat
    From the Personal to the Universal

THREE

    BUILDING A CONTAINER 27

        Some Particulars of Containment

        The Form of a Meeting

        Some Specific Activities

        Drumming

        Joining or Starting a Group

        New Members

        Storms which Threaten the Group

        Brotherhood and Friendship

        Being Lost

APPENDIX

    RESOURCES FOR MEN IN RITUAL GROUPS 43

The purpose of ritual is to wake up the old mind in us, to put it to work. The old ones inside us, the collective unconscious, the many lives, the different eternal parts, the senses and the parts of the brain that have been ignored. Those parts do not speak English. They do not care about television. But they do understand candlelight and colors. They understand nature.

—Z. Budapest

INTRODUCTION

It is terribly important for a man to have some way to continue throughout his life working and playing with male companions who earnestly try to develop personal as well as collective soul. Without some sense of genuine group, too easily the individual man falls asleep or gives up. The history of men, of animals, and of learning has to do with groups, with common effort. A man can risk more exploration of his potentials and of his grandiosity—he can risk more encounters with *grandeur*—when connected to other men who can reduce him when necessary and encourage him when needed.

Wayne Liebman's book poses crucial questions about the formation of small groups, forcing those who seek a group to make basic determinations. Are they simply looking for support and a therapeutic process? Or do they want the opportunity to struggle into a ritual alliance with no guarantee that their therapeutic needs will be filled in the group?

Liebman is writing about groups at the edge, not at the center. In fact, the very idea of a "men's center," named by a city or a state, can be an inflation. To imagine oneself at the center may encourage ego-centricity; it identifies a group with what is known, what is certain, and can lead to what is simply dogmatic. It also promotes a fantasy of healing and redeeming other men, instead of acknowledging that the road is one of discovery, of unearthing, of risk.

1

The great value of *Tending the Fire* is that it positions the ritual group at the edge of society, so that the group may push the personal edges of each man in it. At the core of the group is ambiguity, the uncertain, the as-yet-unformed. So this is not a "how to" book, but one which challenges men to create their own forms, to ask themselves the hardest questions, and invites them to reach into art, their own memories, imagination and skills to enlarge their sense of their own souls as individuals and as men.

I have known Wayne and the men of his group for many years. I admire the tenacity of their struggle to reclaim the domain of myth and ritual as a force in their lives. I applaud Wayne for his attempt to find a language that does not over-simplify, and which describes what this kind of group does without sensationalizing it. His naming these groups "ritual groups" expands the sense of what they are. Although the archetype of initiation (i.e., separation, ordeal and experimentation, then return to the community) underlies the work with ritual, the ritual groups neither pretend to nor offer initiation. Initiation is not a function of a group's intention, it's a function of separation and of the awakening of spirit and soul.

Like a band of hunters or a pack of animals, the ritual group is sustained by the willingness to wander along the uncertain edges of its terrain. It is there that the game is exposed, and will, like the red-eared Stag in Arthurian legend, lead the group on a wild chase, moving ever closer to the center of the forest. As in the animal pack or hunting band, the ritual group protects and nurtures all its members, yet benefits by uncovering and then encouraging the extraordinary capacities in each—this one sees better at night, that one is faster, and so on. If the metaphor for the group is *hunting game in the forest of the soul*, then it's the unusual, the rare, the abnormal, the extreme in each man that will develop from the uncertainty of the pursuit.

—*Michael Meade*

ONE

*It is a massive
masculine shadow,
fifty males sitting together
in hall or crowded room,
lifting something indistinct
up into the resonating night.*

—Robert Bly

LOOKING FOR IRON JOHN

In May, 1983, I returned home to Los Angeles after spending a week with Robert Bly and sixty men in Mendocino, California. I now look back on this week as a pivotal moment in my life, during which I began to heal a wound that I had received as a child through the early death of my father. Although I was a physician with a successful career I felt strangely lacking. It was as if growing up without a father had denied me many experiences that other boys had had, disqualifying me from ever knowing what a real man was.

The week had called up from some part of me a turbulent, generative maleness that was, until that time, completely foreign to my character. Even more remarkably, I had a direct sense—not just a realization—that this maleness was part of something larger and more significant than myself; it had not only to do with other men, but with animals, nature and mythology. Yet scarcely had it begun when the week was over. I wanted more of what I felt in Mendocino, I wanted more depth in my relationships with men, and I wanted this as part of the way I lived day to day.

I went back to Los Angeles eager to interact with men in the feeling way I had in Mendocino. Whereas before I had kept my distance from other men, reacting to them out of fear and mistrust, now I felt a sense of oneness with them that I wanted to maintain. Unfortunately, Bly had led very few conferences for men then and I didn't know anyone in Los Angeles who had been to one. I tried to tell the men I knew about what happened, but I couldn't find words for how the mythology and ritual at Mendocino had affected me. Of course I looked forward to going back to Mendocino again, but what was I to do until then? It seemed I had landed on a marvelous new continent, but now there was a sign on the beach saying, "Closed until next year." I didn't want my link to the mythological world to be a once a year affair. The change I felt in myself was vital and immediate, and I wanted a group of men in my life who felt the same thing in themselves.

Later that year I worked to organize a five-day conference for men with Robert Bly and Michael Meade in Temescal Canyon, Los Angeles. The conference took place in January, 1984 and thirty-five men attended. On the last day I spoke about my desire to be part of a group of men who wanted to continue to work mythologically and ritually among themselves. I asked if others were interested in such a group. A month later ten of us began meeting fortnightly in a converted garage at the back of my house.

Bly believed that many difficulties of men were dilemmas of mythology created by a culture unconscious of its tie to myth. Through storytelling, poetry, ritual and drumming he and Michael helped to create a climate in which we had opened our hearts as men. Now Robert and Michael were gone. Our problem was to create and preserve the same conditions for ourselves. We didn't know how to do this, if we could, or what obstacles lay in our path. We did sense the rightness of our desire.

At the time we began none of us anticipated the difficulty of using ritual to inspire and retain for ourselves an experience of masculinity in our everyday lives. We needed to understand that our emotional natures were a part of being men, that feelings we were more accustomed to hiding than revealing were actually our entry to a relationship with what was deeply male in us. These were lessons from larger men's gatherings which we apparently needed to re-learn in an intimate, continuing group that had no leader.

Four years and many detours later the group we started in Temescal Canyon began sponsoring events for other men in Los Angeles. This step seemed a natural outgrowth of our struggles, a way to further support our own work and to give back something of what this work had opened for each of us as men. Inspired by a detail from the *Iron John* story—the dog pulled down into the pond—we took a name that seemed to fit, Lost Dog Men's Council. As of this writing, the "Lost Dogs" have been meeting seven years. There are currently eleven members, seven from the original group.

In the decade since Bly first began leading workshops for men, there has been an accelerating appreciation for ritual and mythology as vehicles of manhood. I believe the small ritual group helps to make these new-old modalities widely available to men. The small group generates a local community in which men can safely wrestle with the most difficult questions of what it means to be male. Moreover, the group applies these questions to the members' lives as they are living them.

Over the years men occasionally approached our group and asked to join. Sometimes we could say yes, but more often we were already at our limit, and we knew of no other groups in Los Angeles like ours to refer them to. I started keeping a list of men who wanted to be in a ritual men's group and began to put these men in touch with one another. I would meet with some of these new groups two or three times to share some of the missteps and successes of the Lost Dog group. Currently I know of more than a dozen such ritual groups in Los Angeles, each of about ten men.

Recently some men asked me to set down my thoughts about the purpose, organization and function of a ritual men's group. I think, on balance, there are some practical things to say to men who want to bring more of the benefit of ritual into their lives. But I have two strong reservations about doing this. My difficulties in communicating my experience of men's gatherings have convinced me that something happens in ritual that can't be put into words. The strength of ritual, its center, is ultimately sacred and mysterious. Writing about it does not contain the juice of it. Worse, it may trivialize and open it to ridicule.

Secondly, while suggestions about organizing a ritual group can be helpful to interested men, it's a mistake to accept a prescription for going about it. The test of value for a particular structure, ritual, poem or story is whether (and in what way) it is affecting those who participate in it. The question men continually want to ask in this work is not if what they do is in accord with some outside authority or agenda, but is it in accord with themselves? Is the experience, *right now*, giving them a stronger connection to what makes them feel more like men? If the answer is yes, they're doing something right. Each must resolve this for himself again and again. What follows are my reflections on what has and hasn't worked both for myself and for some groups with which I am acquainted.

The Nature of the Ritual Group

The focus of a ritual men's group is mythological. The group enables its members, for a limited time in a protected space, to enter what some have called the mythological world (which I will describe more fully in the next section). Through their interaction with this world, men feel an authenticity in their place as men. The ritual group is spiritual in the fullest sense; it honors each man's most deeply felt truth. Responding to the thread of psychic life that is shared by all men, the group validates each man as a unique embodiment of maleness.

The small ritual groups are not affiliated with any organization or religion. The membership is a collection of peers. There is no leader and no one is paid. I believe that the lack of a leader makes the ritual group more, rather than less, powerful. There is a tendency to give authority and confidence over to a leader. In the ritual group the leader is inside, and each man has the responsibility for making a relationship with him.

The ritual group builds on the work of what are known as "process" or "therapy" groups. Both the ritual and process group invite deep feeling. Both are receptive to the concerns that men have, seek to heal the emotional numbness men often feel and attempt to validate their inner lives. The two groups differ in the way they deal with feeling. The process group emphasizes the feeling life of men as individual human beings; the ritual group emphasizes the feeling life of men *as men*, pointing to something deep within and yet greater than their individual selves.

Though the ritual and process group complement one another, I think it's a mistake to try to combine both functions in one group. It tends to work out best if men forming a group agree in advance on which type they want. It's valuable for the ritual group if the men in it have an awareness of psychological processing, for example, from therapy or counseling, and know the difference between process and ritual. Inevitably, a certain amount of processing occurs within the ritual group; the more aware the members are of their needs and projections, the more capable they are of listening to the needs of others, the less time will be consumed by personal difficulties. The main focus of a ritual group, however, is not processing but developing a connection between what is personal in the members' lives to what is universal in the lives of men.

Mythological Reality and the Container of the Ritual Group

The term "mythological" refers to the realm of human experience that reveals itself in images and stories. The stories—myths and fairy tales—depict themes of eternal concern to men and women. Mythological reality contrasts with ordinary reality. Ordinary reality pertains to the level of daily life. It comprises the physical world which we see, hear and touch. Mythological reality comprises the world of stories, and refers to the level from which we make sense of daily life.

Myths are universal and impersonal, yet they touch us individually by articulating some invisible theme or drama that goes on under the surface of seemingly routine life. For example, growing up without a father had left me with a feeling I was in some way incomplete as a man. When I was an adult, I heard the Grimms' fairy story about Iron John, the strange, hairy man from the bottom of the pond who carried the king's son into the forest. The story reminded me of my own life, of my childhood longing for an older male who would take me under his wing. But the story did more than that. It also told me that my longing was for something richer than I knew, that my longing was shared by other men, and that my life no longer needed to be a dead end in this regard. The story had a quality of redemption. It changed the way I looked at my life.

When we perceive an event mythologically, that event cannot be seen as insignificant or foolish. Rather, any experience (viewed from mythological perspective) is a meaningful

9

drama with a purpose and a message. The Lost Dog group, for example, chose its name to encapsulate the feeling of being pulled down by something dark and mysterious. On the mythological level, the group is one organism, and each individual's circumstance is one aspect of that organism. The experience of everyone in the group is valid beyond question, concerns the whole and helps the whole to reveal itself.

Though the mythological world is as psychically valid as the concrete world, it can't be seen, heard or touched. Mythological reality is evoked through metaphor, as an "as if," using art, poetry, dance, storytelling, or ritual as the vehicles which bring it to awareness. Mythological reality is inhabited by gods, goddesses, kings, queens, warriors, magicians, hermits, witches, dwarves, fools, animals, spirits, demons, monsters and other fairy tale folk. These characters are not human, yet they are alive and real in the sense that they hold place in the human psyche. The closer you come to feeling these mysterious beings alive within yourself, the more sense of sacredness you feel. When you enter their world—confront them on their terms—they will affect you and you will emerge from the encounter renewed, defeated, enriched, diminished, uplifted, perplexed, amazed, or altered in some way.

I believe a primary concern of the ritual group is the construction and preservation of a container for mythological experience. The "mythological container" is a vessel which allows the participants to identify and elaborate the mythological themes in their lives, to appreciate themselves in relation to the mythological world. When the ritual group is working right it protects, encloses and supports the mythological world through the joined physical, intellectual, emotional and spiritual effort of the members. In return, the container opens the members to a dimension of life that extends beyond a subjective understanding of self. The energy of myth brings a sense of inclusiveness, belonging, coherence and purpose; it is soul-sustaining and soul-empowering, giving resilience to live and create in a civilization that often seems valueless and bent on destroying.

Our sense of relation to the mythological world is a fragile one. It needs the structure of a container to preserve it. Otherwise it disappears. In antiquity there were many containers—mystery schools, sacred sites, temples, an exuberant religious life. In such an atmosphere the mythological world flourished and was a force in the lives of women and men; in our technological age few containers remain. Containment is therefore the lifeblood of the ritual group. When the container—in whatever form and by whatever rules a given group establishes it—is honored, the group upholds the seriousness of its intentions toward the inner world. Yet despite its importance the ritual container itself is not something sacred; the container merely embodies the group's best conception of how to invite sacredness to happen.

TWO

When the bond between
heaven and earth is broken
even prayer is not enough;
only a story can mend it.

—The Baal Shem Tov

INVITING THE MYTHOLOGICAL

An hour after sunset ten men gather in a dark room. They sit in a circle on the floor in the center of which is a lit candle. Next to it lies a bowl of burning sage. The odor of sage surrounds them, washes over them, recalls them to a time when the land on which this house was built was a vast prairie. No one speaks. The only sound is the measured breath of one man, then another, then another. They inhale the sweet smell of sage and breathe it out again, and in their mingled exhalation a shadowy outline forms. Some nights it is the shadow of a raven, or coyote, or feather. Some nights it is nothing at all. Tonight it is a man, who sits three feet above the flame. His arms are black, covered in mud, and extend downward. Nobody sees him. Nobody sees his head nod slightly. At length one man begins to speak.

Working Mythologically

The ritual men's group is a vessel which clears a place for the extraordinary in a man's life and so awakens his imagination to it. When this happens, his life is no longer just his life, but the characterization of a larger story telling itself through him. Every man has a story to tell. An advantage of a small ritual group over a conference is that it allows each man and all the men together more time to work with their stories. Through a variety of methods, each man's specific material becomes a vehicle for the group to touch the more general theme it contains. For example, one man may tell a story of heartache about his relationship with his father. This may stir the other men to tell their stories about how it is for them with their fathers—what are the pitfalls, the challenges, the rewards. Out of the group sharing comes a sense of how men encounter "father" in their lives. The group may go on to note parallels between their stories and some myths and fairy tales which are thousands of years old, and which link them to a community of men over time.

So the story moves from the individual to the group to the universal. The story becomes about what fathering means and is, what the maleness in the relationship between father and son is. Each man feels himself living out part of the theme of maleness, and the theme living itself out in him. He is thinking about himself mythologically rather than psychologically, and the significance of this is not that it gives answers to problems, or even that it compels creative responses to problems, but that it fosters a sense of partnership with the mysterious forces of the universe. The man who first told about his father related a story of heartache which initially detracted from his sense of being a man, and which now confirms that he is a man. His emotional nature—this time his sorrow, another time his joy—is part of his being a man. It's part of how he knows himself, and instead of suffering or running from it, he grows more accepting of it and begins to bring it with him without reservation to the tasks of his life.

In a ritual group, the point in working with personal material is always to probe its mythological core, to treat it mythologically by taking it first into the realm of the group and then into the mythological world. The group will ask itself over and over, "How does what this man has said extend beyond his own situation? How do we work mythologically with this?"

The Talking Stick

The talking stick is a Native American tool that helps to create a sacred space for exchanging ideas. The tradition is to carve or decorate a special piece of wood that becomes a ritual object for the group. When there are hard things to talk about the stick is passed around the circle. Holding the stick confers on a man the authority to be heard; it's his time to speak his truth and have it listened to without being cut off, without the discussion spilling out into a free-for-all. More than this, the stick empowers a man to talk in a particular, focused way, in which he digs down and offers the group the inmost essence of himself. When someone takes the stick in his hands the room grows quiet, the mood changes, everyone descends. A man has a form in which to speak about anger or fears which may otherwise be unspeakable.

It works like this: one man takes the stick and speaks. The others keep silent and listen. There are three rules. Speak briefly. Speak about yourself. Speak from your heart. Suppose (as sometimes happens) there is anger in the group. In such a case it's not okay for a man to take the stick and say, "You're an asshole," to someone else, because he's not to speak about someone else: he's to speak about himself. It is okay for a man to say to another, "I'm so mad at you I could kill you," first because now he's talking about himself, but more importantly because now he's encapsulating for the group the depth of his anger. He's telling the group that the other man has pushed him to the edge, and that inside he feels as if it's his life or the other man's. By doing so he's contained his anger rather than spilled it, and he gains a larger sense of himself. All men know such rage and vulnerability and it terrifies them. To speak freely of it is to begin to own it as part of what being a man means.

When the first man finishes, he passes the stick to the man next to him, and so it goes. The stick always moves around the circle, never across. If you have remarks you feel you can't contain and you don't have the stick in hand, you contain them anyway. If you have nothing to say or if someone has already said what you wanted to say, just pass the stick to the next man when it gets to you. By the end of a round pretty much everything that can be said about something has been said. Rarely a man will request another round and the group decides "yes" or "no."

The talking stick is useful for all kinds of issues, especially the ones that get everyone excited. Maybe a particularly charged topic has been chosen that evening—say, "What scares me most about women," or "The thing I feel I failed at." Other times the need for discussion will arise unplanned—a man asks for some help, a problem arises in the group, etc. In taking the stick, the men turn the act of looking for their individual truths into a process which unifies them.

Responding to Myths, Fairy Stories, Dreams and Personal Dramas

Another way of taking the group to a more compelling level of male experience is for a man to bring the group a story that he's drawn to. Maybe he's working with his anger and has found a story with anger in it; maybe something in the story puzzles or fascinates him and he doesn't know why.

This man would spend some time alone with the story, perhaps waiting for a turn to tell it. Memorizing the story (not reading from a written text) seems important. By learning a story, a man mixes it more with his body, "incorporating" it into himself.

In his work at the larger men's conferences, Michael Meade has developed a way of responding to stories on their own terms which is adaptable in small groups. This technique takes men directly into the mythological realm of the story, from which perspective their personal lives appear different. The method involves each man listening to the story and selecting from it the detail that is most striking to him.

The detail someone picks is his entrance into the story, where the story becomes real and alive for him, where he most strongly identifies with it. The detail can be anything from the story—something someone said, a question, dilemma or impossible task, a place, an article of clothing, a building or an object, an animal, the color of someone's eyes, a situation a particular character finds himself in, or something one of the characters does or sees. The detail chosen may puzzle, anger, delight, horrify, fascinate, terrify, sadden, etc. Whatever the detail is or does, it carries special significance for the man who chooses it. The more strongly the detail reverberates in him, the more the story will open itself.

Next the men may rearrange themselves in the circle according to the order in which their particular details

18

occurred. Then, starting with the detail that came first in the story, each man shares his detail with the group. He doesn't analyze why his detail seems important to him, doesn't talk about his problems in psychological terms. He simply describes his detail and the impact it has on him, how it makes him feel, as vividly as he can. Then he may name the moment in his life evoked by the detail.

For example, a man might share the shock and dismay he felt when a woman he regarded as his princess turned into a hag; or the impossible challenge now presented at work to climb a mountain as slick as glass. When each man hears the details that others have chosen he hears things about the story that passed him by. The story is an intuitive reservoir whose relevance to the struggles, predicaments and relationships of all the men gradually reveals itself. The story has a flow of its own. The effect of going around the room opens men to perceive beyond their own stumbling blocks. They see what preceded and what lies ahead of where they stopped. They become sensitive to a journey-like quality and ongoing significance to events.

When the evening is over, the men come away with the sense that, as men, they're not only living out their personal lives, but something communal which the story reflects back to them. The story has a particular vitality for each man; it accompanies and supports him wherever he goes. This happens through each man simply focusing on one detail and talking about it as concretely as he can. Curiously, sometimes a man will be hearing a story for a second time, and be struck by a detail that he overlooked before; the whole story will have changed for him.

The story technique has another application, quite apart from myths and fairy tales. Some nights men may speak in the group of their dreams or personal dramas. The method of "finding a detail" provides a supportive way of responding to this material which avoids processing and allows the group to delve into the larger story behind it. For example, if men bring in their dreams for a night of dream telling, each man can respond to a dream of someone else's by treating the dream as if it were a story and speaking about his detail. That is, "This is where I enter your dream, this is the part of your dream that draws out something in me." So each man can answer any other man's personal material as if a story is being told. Each man, by focusing on where he enters the material, addresses it by talking about himself. The effect of all the men doing this is to carry the discussion forward from what is individual in men to what is collective.

Creating Rituals

If a man finds a myth or part of a myth that is telling his story, then he looks for ways to get closer to it, to bring it down into his life and his body. Memorizing and telling the story is one way to do this. Another way is to act a part of it out ritually; using his imagination, a man creates an action which opens him even more to the story, allowing it to resonate more sharply in him. I'd like to make a slight digression to show how an event in my own life corresponded to a mythic theme that later became ritualized for me.

Until I was about thirty-five I couldn't face my mother when she was crying. It was as if her tears cast a spell over me and I would promise her anything she wanted to get her to stop. One night I quit doing that. She came over to talk, began to cry, and instead of reassuring her that I would take care of her by doing the things she wanted, I just held her and told her I understood how bad she was feeling. That night I had a dream in which Jung appeared with a small furnace in his hands, which he held out to me. I don't think the dream meant that Jung had returned from the spirit world with a message for me. I think my psyche, looking for a metaphor to describe what had happened that night, came up with the image of Jung as the only thing sufficiently startling. Not giving in to my mother's tears was an act so Herculean for me that it was as if I needed the resources of Jung to do it.

About a year later I heard Bly relate the Chinese tradition (told to him by Al Huang) that a man has a small furnace in his abdomen. It is called the Tan Tien (pronounced Don CHEN), and a man uses it to burn his sufferings. The idea is not that by doing so he gets rid of his pain, but that he turns his pain to fuel which makes him stronger. I remembered my dream and was so taken with the image of the small furnace that I wanted to bring it tangibly into my life in some way. When I saw an Oriental lantern that looked like the furnace in my dream, I bought it. I showed it to the men in my group, told them the whole story, and asked if it would be appropriate to light it. They were enthusiastic, and the ritual of lighting the Tan Tien has become a fixture of our meetings.

Discovering stories that speak to all men and acting to give body to these stories is the work of a ritual men's group. The fire that uses suffering for fuel is an instance of a mythological motif that has meaning in the lives of many men. So the ritual of lighting the lantern can be powerful. An important thing to remember about rituals is that they are metaphoric of interior processes. Thus burning one's pain doesn't literally mean setting fire to the object of your suffering. It isn't my mother or her tears I want to burn; I want to digest them both, to incorporate them as parts of myself so that I can gain strength. The lighting of the Tan Tien helps me to do this.

Feelings and Resistance to Feelings

I used to think it was a particular problem of mine that I had trouble recognizing myself as "manly" when I was full of feeling. I've realized since that it's common for men to have an ambivalence about their feelings, and to feel a loss of identity when they disclose them. The ritual group provides an environment that men come back to again and again in which it's safe to explore what they feel. Men who previously could speak of their feelings only privately and to women can try out what it's like to display their emotions in a more public way before the eyes of other men.

A special power of the ritual group is to relate the feeling life of men to their myths. Myths not only highlight feelings, but also give them meaning. For example when a fairy tale hero is lost and out of chances, he often weeps. The story says this must be the way of men; to grasp this is to gain an emotional benefit from listening to stories mythologically. When men hear one another from this perspective, the feelings they express draw them together. Though the demonstration of a particular feeling may cause apprehension among the group members, it also validates their identities as men. They begin to regard any feeling revealed in the group as a gift, to be given the same respect and attention as if told in a sacred story.

I've noticed there is often a progression that occurs with feelings in groups of men: first a feeling happens, there's an initial response of fear in the room (sometimes this takes the form of talking a man away from his feelings, encouraging him to "fix" his problem), then a slow appreciation for the feeling develops, then everyone feels closer. Ritual groups inevitably take some time learning to move through this. The key is to focus on the acceptance of feelings, rather than to analyze them. If, for example, a man sharing his story detail begins to weep, the others should give him their attention, empathy and time, not their opinions. One convention that is used at the larger conferences is to give a man a simple "ho!" when he's done to tell him he's been received.

Occasionally a man has so much grief or turmoil that he may request (or the group may decide he needs) special time that night. This may provide another opportunity for the group to go down into feeling. But it's important for the men to know that they can be compassionate and still say "no." Moreover it's helpful if the man in need asks for something specific. This means that if someone does want time, he's worked on his problem awhile apart from the group, and has gained a sense of the issues involved below the surface. If he knows what he wants from the others, he's defined a common ground out of which they can respond. The feeling is contained—given a home where it's safe to be uncovered—while enclosed. This increases the prospect that one man's troubles not only won't consume the group's energy, but will likely contribute to it.

Turning Up the Heat

A group can make the right moves, create a lasting, supportive vessel and feel very snug and safe. The stronger the container, the hotter the flame it can withstand; the hotter the flame the more mythological essence can be extracted from raw personal material. Thus the container has meaning in relation to what the men bring to it. If they bring nothing in for burning, then the container exists for nothing. By this I mean that if men don't prepare to risk themselves personally, little will happen in the ritual group. What is the point of bringing in a story to tell, a poem to recite, a dance to dance, unless you have first made it yours by living it? Otherwise these are empty forms, repeated for the sake of repeating. What is the point of talking about issues in the language of others? Only when you find your own language to describe your life does the language have power.

One night in the Lost Dog group a man was talking about how scary it was for him at work. His boss was like a Grand Inquisitor, putting everyone on trial for the most trivial mistakes. Then the man excused himself and went out the door. A minute later someone else returned, a hooded figure with a white, distorted face, who began shrieking at us. This was no human being, but a creature from the darkness of this man's imagination. He began to accuse us, one by one, with his words. As if he had a thousand eyes, he knew all the points of male vulnerability. He terrified us, especially when he extended the sword he held in his hands. The man had taken the risk of letting his own Grand Inquisitor into the room and facing the reactions of the other men.

The moment of the Grand Inquisitor was a particularly serious one for our group. There have been other moments when the spirit was light—moments, for example, when coyote appeared with his tricks. These visitations come not out of a man's wanting to entertain or instruct, but from his asking himself, with all the courage he can muster, what is true in his life, where he is hurting, where he is overflowing, what does he need right now, where is the piece of him that is missing. He risks an articulation of his confusion, his anger, his joy, his non-resolution, his I've-had-it-up-to-here. This articulation is more than a sharing of his personal feelings, as might occur if the group's emphasis were on processing or support; rather, it's a reach into the part of himself brushed by divine forces. Though he may never fully comprehend the totality there, he never stops pursuing, valuing or contending with it. He brings to the group the portion of himself that he encounters not with the idea of finding completion, but with the idea of including the group as he grapples with the fundamental questions in his life. So each man's wound is his personal gate into the mytho-logical world, and when he stays present with his wound and goes through the gate as this man did, he brings back an experience of the mythological that touches every man in his core. The personal doesn't stay personal, and all go further together than one might have gone alone.

From the Personal to the Universal

The Grand Inquisitor story is an example of a man who took a personal risk in the group. In trying to penetrate his experience to the core, he discovered and acted out for the group a character inside himself. He took what had been an interpersonal problem and made it *intra*personal, relating it to the development of his manhood. The group provided a focus for a kind of observation and enactment that he couldn't do alone.

I want to say more about how to take personal material to a more universal level. I'd like to illustrate the steps a man might go through to do the same thing with a story. Say a man in a group, lets call him Tom, has a problem in his marriage: he's become sexually estranged from his wife and they have not made love for several months. Whenever he tries to initiate lovemaking, she puts him off with vague excuses. Tom doesn't talk about the problem easily, in fact he feels a sense of shame and failure as a man because of it. So he keeps silent. One day he happens to hear a reference to the mythological character Rhiannon, a beautiful woman on horseback who rides past a group of men. When they give chase she speeds up, remaining out of reach. When they slow down she slows down, keeping the distance between them constant. Tom is struck by the image of a woman constantly just out of reach. He looks up the story ("Pwyll" in the *Mabinogion*) and learns it. Somehow the image of Rhiannon contains the essence of the frustration he feels in his marriage; he'd like to probe further. One night in the group Tom tells the story. "I'd like you to imagine Rhiannon," he says, "And I'd like each of you to see if there's an experience of Rhiannon in your life."

In a therapy group Tom might talk about his problem and receive feedback. But in the ritual group he tells a mythological story and asks the group to relate it to their own lives. As each man speaks, Tom hears how the story reverberates in ways he hadn't imagined. When the evening is over, he goes home not only feeling closer to the men in his group, but with new respect for the Rhiannon in his life, the one inside for whom he sometimes mistakes his wife. However he approaches the situation in his relationship, and whatever his wife's response, his perspective has changed and the old problem isn't the same. From feeling isolated and inadequate, he's moved to a different way of understanding, and perhaps to a new level of confidence in facing his feelings of frustration.

The same principle of penetrating the experience operates whatever the group does. Men who want a sweat lodge, for example, could pay an "expert" to provide it for them. But they also might gather volcanic rock themselves, cut down and bind wild willow to construct the lodge, build their own fire. By doing these things with their own hands they would be circling the essence they seek in the lodge, deepening their relationship to it. When a group penetrates something by looking for the core of truth it holds for them in common, they cross a threshold into the mythological world. They begin to spiral around it and in response it gives them something which alters them, and which they take with them.

THREE

Start a huge, foolish project, like Noah.
It makes absolutely no difference
what people think of you.

—Rumi

BUILDING A CONTAINER

Since the group's relationship with the mythological world is both precious and vulnerable, it becomes important for them to safeguard it by considering certain details of containment. When I first began to think about the idea of a container for the group, I thought it odd. The image of containment is distinctly feminine—something which holds, nourishes, encloses and protects. It's very different from the kind of constructions we usually associate with men and boys—edifices, towers, swords. Yet by the enigmatic act of men creating a container the group perpetuates itself. I'm sure that something deeply unifying happens inside each man as he grapples to develop this shepherding, caretaking function in the absence of women. I believe he learns something that he can only learn from other men, and which is vital for his life and relationships.

Some Particulars of Containment

One early discussion the group might want to have is about the level of confidentiality that will best promote their being open with one another. Assuring a fundamental ground of trust will enable the men to speak more freely about their circumstances, their ideas and their feelings without fear that their words will travel outside the group.

They also may want to agree on the way in which confidentiality will apply to their rituals and practices. For example,

29

I think it's good, when asked, to share in a general way about the group to interested men and women. But too much sharing among inappropriate company can lessen the group's momentum both for yourself and the other members. The fairy tales employ the metaphor of "showing your gold too soon" when describing how the immature male demeans his experience by showing it off to others when his real task is to value it himself.

The need for lodge or sanctuary should be given some attention and thought. A private, indoor, permanent home for the group seems to help harness and center the force of the mythological world. When a group meets in the same place time after time that place becomes special to them and contributes to the power of the group. Possibly they will be free to leave ritual objects in the room or close by—a lantern, sage basket, smudge bowl, talking stick, masks, artwork, etc. A living room which isn't vulnerable to interruption by others (no ringing phones), and which doesn't give the group the feeling they are intruding on anyone else, can work well. Likewise a workroom in one man's house. Even a garage can become magical. Pull out the cars, throw down an old rug, hang blankets from the rafters to enclose a space and light a candle in the middle.

The way membership is defined also influences the container. Some men's groups (often called "councils" or "lodges") are open each time to all comers. Usually these are fairly large gatherings (ten to fifty men or more) which meet once a month or so in a public facility. These groups seek to recreate the atmosphere of a men's conference and give the participants a feeling of community. This environment is necessarily less intimate than that of the small ritual group. The small group has about ten members, plus or minus two or three, and meetings are open only to members.

Here are other details which the members might consider ironing out to ease their group's accomplishing what they want it to: (1) Scheduling: It's important to pick a day, time and length of time to meet that everyone can stick to. The frequency of meetings also should feel right to everyone—an interval short enough to maintain the unity, long enough to keep the urgency. (2) Attendance: It's helpful if all the members agree on some minimum standard that keeps the continuity and depth of their work intact, including what a man should do if he's going to skip a meeting. One way some groups deal with this is to ask that a man who is going to miss a meeting get word in advance to another member (it's useful if each man has a printed roster of the membership with addresses and phone numbers.) (3) Punctuality and time: How important is it to the group to start and end on time, and how are they going to see to this? How is ritual time going to be separated from ordinary time? What happens when someone is late, or late repeatedly, or isn't ready to go into ritual time?

It's hard for men to stay focused keeping a priority on their inner lives, and the container of a ritual group will periodically be tested. Distractions occur which not only create difficulties for some members, but also diminish the group's mythological focus. To keep a group centered in the right place, doing the right thing, according to the members' own inner compass, is intense work. Some rules and structures help (and may even be essential), but only the group can say which rules and structures are right for itself at any given time. The process of deciding is ongoing. When the men take the container for granted it can become leaky and the group may have a harder time sustaining its bond to mythological reality. When the men are mindful of their needs for structure, the group as a whole begins to feel the container as a concentrating force designed by their own effort, to which they are committed by virtue of authorship.

The Form of a Meeting

Early in the life of a ritual group, the men may worry about what to do at a meeting, and whether they're doing it right. Though ideas and guidelines are often helpful, I want to stress again the importance of a group's developing its own form out of its feelings, needs and preferences. There is no "proper" way for a meeting to unfold, nothing required of the men beyond attending to the quality of their experience. If things go well on a given night, then the group will be in touch awhile with how the mythological world is manifesting in them. If not, and the group feels out of touch with their purpose, then it will be important for them to review what they are doing and consider changes. This in mind, here are a few thoughts on form borrowed from the Lost Dog group and others I know of.

Although the ritual group is leaderless it needs direction. I've spent a lot of time in groups shooting the breeze, everyone secretly hoping the meeting would somehow start itself. One way to help the group fix its bearings is to designate in advance one man each meeting to "hold the container." This man functions as the "ritual elder" who orchestrates the evening, protects its structure and keeps the group on track. It's his job to say "It's time to start," "Is everyone finished with this?" etc. It's also the ritual elder's job to plan something for the group based on his particular capacities and his sense of the group's direction. He might tell a story, or conduct a meditation or a chant, or guide a poetry or dream session, or lead a discussion around the circle about a subject that is meaningful for him and that he senses would be meaningful for the group.

"Holding the container" impels a man toward a sense of stewardship for the group. It encourages him to take the development and preservation of the container seriously. It's not only the group's container, it's his container, and his work and the group's work are tied together. The position can rotate each time. One simple way is to move through the group roster in alphabetical order. This gives each man time to think about what he wants to lead the group in and permits him to notify the others in advance if, for example, he wants them to come prepared with a dream or poem.

A few minutes before the formal start of the evening, some groups take time to socialize over coffee or tea. The ritual elder, if there is one, might signal when it's time to begin. There may be announcements ("There's a good article in this or that journal,") and logistics ("Next meeting falls on a holiday so we need to talk about changing the date,") followed by a check-in.

A check-in is a quick once around in which each man tells the others what's happening in his life—I'm having a good week, my girlfriend and I are fighting, etc. (It's a good idea to apply a fairly strict time limit, say one or two minutes, to protect against the evening getting consumed in this way.) The check-in is a means of honoring the natural concern and affection that the members have for one another. It lets everyone know at the outset what's uppermost in everyone's mind. This has several benefits: it puts a boundary around the personal material. It may be the first time all day a man has checked in with himself. It also may be that what's going on in one man will affect the group later that night.

The next step is to edge away from the outer world. It helps if each man can take a step down into his feelings. Some groups have a second round, an "inner" check-in, expressly for that purpose. Usually once the anecdotes are out it's easier to get to the feelings. You can do it in a word, better yet a sound. The "inner" check-in is a statement of what things feel like on the inside, no story attached. When you've gotten to the feelings the "inner" check-in is over. If you're feeling frustration because something is going on with you and you can't articulate what it is, that's a fine check-in, too.

To help shift the mood out of ordinary time, it's useful to make a physical change at some point—stand up and stretch, dim the lights, sound an instrument, etc. This is also a good moment for an opening ritual. In many groups the ritual elder smudges everyone with burning sage. Smudging is a Native American tradition, in which smoke is wafted (usually with a feather) over each man. The intent is that as the smoke washes over you it momentarily cleanses you of your outside cares. After the ritual elder has smudged everyone the last man smudges him. Some groups sit in silence awhile afterward, others chant or drum. The attempt here is to feel sacred time, and there is no hurry.

Throughout the meeting, the ritual elder holds an awareness that the group needs a sense of where it is, although he himself may not always know. So he doesn't simply present what he's planned. He asks—"Would it feel right if we did this now?" The group proceeds by consensus. Maybe something unexpected has come up—for example, a death in one man's family. The ritual group is an ideal place to take a personal event of this magnitude and use it as a vehicle for all the men to strengthen their connection. The men choose whatever form feels best—pass the talking stick, improvise a ritual of healing, etc.

There is often a ritual to close, such as the "naming" ritual that ends some larger conferences: The men rise and stand in a circle with their arms around one another. When the first man is ready he says, "My name is ___." The group responds "Your name is ___," and repeats the name twice more. Then the man next to him says his name in the same way, the group responds to him, and so on. Sometimes you feel apprehensive leaving the intimacy of sacred space to re-enter ordinary time. The naming ritual reaffirms your identity in the outer world as you move away from the inner one.

Some Specific Activities

I hope it's evident that the sense of what to do on any given night emerges from the needs of the group and the individuals in it, not from a list. I've never been able to know in advance how a group is going to get from concrete reality to the mythological level. Some nights a word, a gesture, or just sitting in silence unlocks the door to the other world. You try to open your heart and do the things you feel are right. You do them with attention and respect and hope for the best. Here are some modes through which the door sometimes opens: storytelling; poetry; dream sharing; meditation; movement; song; chanting; prayer; drumming; dancing; hugging, holding and lifting; dancing or reciting poetry to drums; working in clay or other media; mask making; face painting; howling at the moon; playing musical instruments or recorded sacred music; reading from selected writers; showing slides; reading a play by taking parts; sharing soul stories; holding a sweat lodge; devising rituals for specific purposes—for example, a ritual of passage for a man who plans to marry.

One way a group of men feels closer is by talking about concerns that all males share. Here are some that seem to surface repeatedly: your relationship to your work; how you feel about sex; how you feel about your mother and father, your father's work, your father's failings, your brothers or sisters, your children, your friendships, your lover or spouse; your perception of God or religion; grandparents; ancestors; failing, failing big, failing to fail big; your relationship to money; your heroes; your success; how you feel about rejection, loneliness; what you're ashamed of; what you feel guilty about; what you believe beautiful and ugly; what you most love, hate and fear; death.

At times, groups feel they are in a rut or need to stretch themselves. Some have special meetings in different places. Others have gone to concerts or poetry readings; climbed a mountain; camped out; created a weekend workshop for themselves; gone stargazing; built something together.

The things I've listed here are no good if done or talked about by rote. What matters is how you come to what you do. If you proceed from the inside out, valuing questions more than answers, the shadowy outline of something remarkable may begin to take shape.

Drumming

Of the many tools available to men doing ritual work, drumming has become the most emblematic. The reason is apparent to anyone who has encountered a group of drummers absorbed in a rhythmic line: the magnetic power of the beat, hand on skin, embodies a vitality that is eternal and available to everyone who listens. It's impossible not to be caught up in it, swayed by it.

Before I met Michael Meade, I thought drumming meant *trap*, the combination of snares, cymbals, etc. that were part of a jazz or rock band. But the drums Michael introduced to the conferences were hand drums from various cultures— Latin *congas*, Turkish *dumbegs*, African *djimbes*. We learned specific rhythms, especially the *Samba*, and layered on other percussive effects with cowbells, tambourines, sticks and rattles. The emphasis on form was important; through it we began to appreciate what drummer Mickey Hart has called "drum's second voice," the inaudible pulse inside the rhythm.

I think drumming has become important to men's groups because it makes the overlap between physical and spiritual immediately palpable. It's an almost perfect form in which to contain and work with feeling. Particularly for the first few years of my group, drumming was extremely valuable. It was the one mode which would consistently take us where we knew we wanted to go. A story or poem might misfire, a discussion might become too heady, but drumming put us back in our bodies, loosened us, got us to move and dance. It seemed to give us a way of feeling together without words.

The more disciplined we got about our drumming the more it gave back; it was as if the rhythms—grandfather, *Samba*, etc.—were imprinted in the psyche waiting for us to physicalize them in sound. When we performed them rightly the rhythms took over and drummed us as one body.

A man may feel sheepish when he first holds a drum, as if the spontaneity a drum nourishes is more appropriate to a child than an adult. Enthusiasm quickly replaces embarrassment, however, especially if a good teacher is on hand the first few times. Many men's gatherings include drumming as an organized activity which builds the sense of community. Some ritual groups new to drumming engage a coach for one or two hours to help them get going.

A group can drum in a variety of ways. They may decide to stay with a specific form such as *Samba*. Or they can improvise, for example by starting with the simple one-two of the grandfather beat and jumping in over it one man at a time. When a group finds their rhythmic line, it's very apparent, very exhilarating. The beat will become a living thing, growing, diminishing, transforming, supporting the group for a long while before dying out.

The energy of the drum can become so quickly compelling for a group that some members may want *only* to drum. Slowly, though, the men become more practiced at telling stories and poems, and more willing to risk articulating their feelings in words and rituals. Drumming remains important, but the vocabulary of ritual expands to include other things. It's a great joy to begin combining forms—for example, an evening of each man telling a poem or dream while the group supports him rhythmically with drums.

Joining or Starting a Group

The most important requirement for those who join a ritual men's group is to have a profound longing to be in a community of men who are seeking to build a partnership with what is uniquely male in themselves. Possibly this means that they will have previously spent some time in ritual with other men. Whatever their background, they would know the value of ritual and mythology for validating what is masculine in their movements, ideas, feelings, desires, perceptions. They would want more of it, regularly, and would be willing to make some sacrifices of time and energy to get it.

If the groups in your area are full, you can start one yourself. A good time to get a new group going is just after a several-day men's conference. These gatherings inspire men with a sense of kinship. As the validity of the mythological world strikes men they see its relevance to their lives and may discover a need to increase their involvement in it. If you're at a conference and want to be in a ritual group, stand up and say so. The likelihood is that there are other men living near you who share your desire. One man I know didn't want to wait for a conference, put a flyer out at the local Jung Institute, and was inundated with calls.

If you know some men who have been in a ritual group for a while you might consider inviting one or two to an early meeting of your group to share their experiences. Men in a new group seem to find this helpful and reassuring. It's also personally rewarding for the men you invite.

If no men in your community are familiar with mythological work, you can generate interest by selectively sharing some of your experiences and passing around articles and tapes (such as the 1989 Bly/Moyers interview on PBS). If you know a man interested in learning more about ritual and mythology, encourage him to read and to attend some workshops and conferences. He'll approach you if he decides he wants to join a group. Another way to engage men is to ask a presenter from a larger men's conference to come to your area. Many of these speakers make their living conducting weekend workshops for men and are available.

Finally, you can simply start a poetry or story or movement (or anything else) group for men you know. No need to talk about men's work, the Wildman or any questions of masculinity. Men who meet for the sake of their love of beauty or art or craft will develop an enthusiasm for being together.

New Members

When a new group forms there's a period of shifting, a month or two perhaps, as the men decide if it's for them. When the dust clears and ten or so have made a commitment the group might consider closing its membership for around a year to give itself time to gel. From time to time men will move on or move away, opening space for new members.

New blood is invigorating but also disruptive. The group will feel when it's right to look for a new man. This is a tricky area, in which feelings are liable to be hurt both within and outside the group. It's therefore best if the members agree in advance among themselves on how they will proceed. In my own group, for example, we occasionally invite guests. This is a way for men to meet without putting pressure on anyone, and keeps the process of choosing a new member ongoing within the group. When a space does open, we have an idea of some men who may be a good match. We limit our consideration to men who have sought out the opportunity to join and who are well known to more than one member.

Storms Which Threaten the Group

Although I've tried to spell out the importance of the container for ritual work, and the need to be vigilant about those things which can slow the group down, I feel compelled to mention that sometimes difficulties of an even more serious nature arise. Occasionally, problems surface which may so shake the group as to jeopardize its survival. I've called these "storms which threaten the group." It might take every bit of everyone's energy and endurance to weather them, but if the vessel makes it through it will be stronger.

For a variety of reasons and on any given night, the personal needs of one or more men may compete with the group's mythological intentions. Sometimes this happens in ways which are particularly difficult to handle. Once in a while a man whose private concerns are overpowering him will present the group with a demand for attention that it cannot or does not want to meet. Sometimes a grudge will develop between two men in the group. This may be something that started outside the group, which now intrudes on meetings. Sometimes a man may slowly lose touch with his motivation for being in the group and his indifference may frustrate the other members. The issue is not that men have personal or emotional needs. Needs simply are. The issue is, what is the group going to do about *these* needs at *this* time.

The problem may be a one-time disturbance which flares up and is settled in one night. Other difficulties may smolder for months. During such a time meetings may either be full of fireworks or fall flat for no apparent reason. The members can take a long while to penetrate the murkiness, see the trouble for what it is and decide what they want to do with it. Even when the question becomes clear a stalemate can persist. Each group needs to create its own balance between individual and group desires. As every situation is unique, groups do this by trial and error.

It helps if a particular problem can be understood as a dilemma of masculinity: there are forces in men which work to drive them apart and out of the inner world. Since one function of the group is to help heal the split in and between men, it's right for the members to go out of their way to work for a reconciliation. Perhaps a ritual can move the focus away from the personal and toward the mythological level. Or, if the participants have a willingness to be confronted about their projections, maybe they can resolve a conflict, or at least clarify the inner forces enough to work on themselves apart from the group.

But it's also right to be leery of making processing a focus of the group's time. The upshot is this: continued division consumes the group in processing and holds them back. They must find closure. When personal troubles become overwhelming, the group needs to decide openly and directly whether these concerns are a proper point of convergence for the group's time and energy, or if those involved ought to seek support for their problems elsewhere.

Sometimes the group's sense of purpose will lead them to make a clean break. For example, if a man wants something from the group which the group is unwilling to give and he cannot contain his resentment, it's time for him to leave. If the group decides it needs something from a man that he cannot provide, it's time for him to look for another group. If there is animosity between two men and one or both can't stop it from spilling out at meetings, then it's time for one or both to go. If a parting is the outcome, the group might consider honoring this with a ritual of severance to contain the fear that inevitably results from such an occasion.

Brotherhood and Friendship

At first I felt awkward among the men in my group, most of whom I had not known before. I wondered who these men were, what they wanted, what they wanted of me; I know others had similar feelings. With time our personal ties increased. We slowly grew to respect and love one another for our capacities and struggles. We cared about each other's happiness and sadness, successes and failures. After a few years we began to feel right, outside group meetings, calling and being called on by one another for counsel, company or solace. We had become brothers.

I believe it's a mistake, though, to assume that friendships will emerge organically and spontaneously out of the milieu of brotherhood. A close friendship takes its own time and has its own chemistry, whether you're in a group with someone or not. You may become friends with some men in your group. But while the men in a ritual group share what they most privately and deeply feel, their intimacy is not purely personal in its intent. Ultimately, they want to move beyond the individual context from which feelings arise and to awaken in themselves a sense of sacred purpose or meaning.

Being Lost

It's said that we've lost all hope of contact with the old ways. That is, whatever rituals of initiation were practiced by the elders on young men in ancient and primitive times are forever beyond our knowing; that even if we did know them they probably would not do us much good since the mythology behind them has ceased to be our mythology, if it ever was. Yet I believe there is a congruency between the men in the modern ritual group and the boys who were led off into the bush by the old men. The ancient experience of initiation surely entailed some element of chaos and terror, some component of being picked out of a safe environment and thrown into alien territory, not knowing what to expect, unable to go back to the familiar ways of doing things, unsure of the new ones. This is precisely the experience of uncertainty we choose in a ritual group. I believe that even as old structures die, the psychic energies behind them remain; they live on to find new forms in which to embody themselves. What matters most is not the form of the ritual, but the intention behind it, the intensity of the longing.

The group that meets for ritual purposes asks its members to surrender something of themselves. They surrender to the discipline of the ritual, to the space where the ritual is performed, to the force in the mythological world which the ritual honors or appeals to. With the surrender comes fear: fear of uncertainty, fear of chaos, fear of buried pain, fear of being vulnerable in front of other men, fear that the group itself will be a failure. It's important to the group's success for each man to hold an awareness that he has fear, that no matter how adept he gets in the group his fear is more or less always with him, and that it resembles the fear of the other men. It's important for each man to take the risk of looking for his fears, experiencing them, defining them specifically, expressing them, finding correspondences to them in stories, looking for rituals to concretize them.

In a strange way, fear is the only guide to be completely trusted. The next step seems always to come out of a place of darkness, out of the tension of not knowing. The crux of "What now?" lies in your own experience, in containing the apprehension of uncertainty and being willing not to know and not to be told.

Through the first year or two of its existence the Lost Dog group groped for direction. We had yet to understand many things. We felt sorry because we had no leader, no wise elder or Iron John with a vision for guiding us out of the swamp of memories, feelings, desires, arguments and regrets we found ourselves in each time we met. There were no rules or models for this work; our culture had ill prepared us to do it. But it was an endeavor on which, for us, everything depended. One evening as we went around the circle each man gave voice to his frustrations and hopes for the group. One man's words have remained with me. It didn't matter to him whether we were lost he said, he was here to be with other men in this way and that was enough. He ended, "And it's true, we don't have a leader. Well, what can we do about that?"

Not having a leader, not being part of any formal men's organization or set of beliefs, being left to glean your way, is the contemporary experience of maleness. The larger conferences are like huge banquets providing a feast of leadership, community, inspiration, ideas and spirit; but they are fleeting. In the heat of the small groups you determine to cook for yourself. Instead of looking to leaders on the outside, you look to the one in you who leads. You build a local community to discover and learn to sustain pieces of your manhood.

When a group of men sit in silence and darkness together, when they drum by candlelight, sometimes it's right and Iron John is in the room; sometimes not. That's what it's like. We are looking to live our sacred connectedness and we can take heart that men of all times have agonized and asked the same question, "Is this right? Is this the way to be men?"

APPENDIX

Freud and Jung
Sources of Myths and Fairy Tales
Interpretations of Myths and Fairy Tales
Inner Work
Poetry and Essays
Literature, Movies and Music
Catalogues and Presses, Periodicals, Men's
Studies, Conferences, Miscellany

To know Tao is not as good as to love it,
and to love it is not as good as to practice it.

—*Confucius*

RESOURCES FOR MEN IN RITUAL GROUPS

I feel strongly that the perspective, leadership and direction of a ritual group must emerge from its members and not from outside authorities if these groups are to be truly vital. Yet I recognize also that the groups are something genuinely new. Even men who have been to many conferences fall silent in the first meetings of a small ritual group; everyone is ready for something to happen, and yet they feel awkward and strangely without resources.

As the Lost Dog group evolved, it seemed to me that the main task we faced concerned how we worked with feeling. We wanted to discover the forms (e.g., drumming, rituals, chanting, poems, stories, etc.) which would provide a vehicle in which to explore our feelings, and so lead us into partnership with forces that were alive and universal within ourselves. The problem was not simply a matter of whether to impose on ourselves forms from outside or to invent new ones. The real question was how to add depth and meaning. Even more importantly, could we discover forms that held the power of change? For example, drumming seems a universal form for groups of men—but how does it work? What does a particular group drum for, and why do they drum in the way they do? Is drumming a means of finding a common ground? Of opening the door to the other world? Of invoking a particular quality or energy? Are there certain ways to drum that help to do these things? How or where do we learn about this?

I've written *Tending the Fire* to reflect my experience that ritual groups call for a spirit of searching, investigating, reflecting. In this spirit, I'd like to offer some resources that have been useful to me. I've seen how much of the following material works its way into group meetings. All of it has in some way provided insight, reassurance or inspiration which challenged my beliefs, attitudes and perceptions about being a man. Although I've tried to give a framework to the material, this list is selective and highly personal, not meant to be comprehensive. But I do hope it helps others in ways it has helped me—to discover forms which deepen feeling, to learn how to think better about form and feeling, to practice with them in the group.

Freud and Jung

Freud illuminated the underground foundations of the psychic house. Jung discovered the house to be part of a buried city. The ritual work I've described emerges from their discoveries, and from the work of their students.

Freud's contributions have been minimized by some, but he was the first to take the unconscious seriously as a field of investigation, forcing a shift in thinking that is now part of how we talk and see. His bibliography is well known and has never been out of print. If you haven't read him, begin with *The Introductory Lectures on Psychoanalysis* and *The Interpretation of Dreams.*

Jung was the disciple turned apostate, who realized the significance of the mythological world to the psyche, and the implications of its collapse. Though at times his writing is obscure, he has several good interpreters: Edward Whitmont (*The Symbolic Quest*, Princeton University Press), Edward Edinger (*Ego and Archetype*, Penguin Books; see also *Anatomy of the Psyche*, Open Court Publishing Company), Jolande Jacobi (*The Psychology of C.G. Jung*, Yale University Press), Marie-Louise von Franz (*C.G. Jung, A Myth In Our Time*, G.P. Putnam and Sons). In *Memories, Dreams, Reflections* (Vintage Books, Random House) and in his section of *Man and His Symbols* (Doubleday & Company), Jung gives his own account of his psychology and its development.

Many "Jung Institutes" have been established to disseminate Jung's work. They usually maintain libraries and bookstores and often host workshops of interest. In the United States there are Jung Institutes in San Francisco, Chicago (Evanston), New York, Boston, Denver, Toronto and Los Angeles. The Dallas Institute, the Minnesota Jung Association, and the San Diego Friends of Jung Center are similar organizations.

I've found it important in groups not to accept Jung's language as a substitute for my experience. For example, Jung refers to the

"Anima" when describing the feminine or "soul" in a man. The Anima is an experience contained in each man, a force he feels alive inside himself when he looks at a pretty girl, hears beautiful music or poetry or watches a cloud; by doing those things with attention, he co-operates with the infinite in himself. Peter Birkhauser, a Swiss artist who was a patient of von Franz's, has produced an extraordinary series of drawings and paintings (*Light from the Darkness*, with commentary by Marie-Louise von Franz, Birkhauser Verlag), in which he has rendered his experience of the psyche into art, giving body to aspects of Jung's psychology.

Sources of Myths and Fairy Tales

There can be many versions of stories, many interpretations. Sometimes a story will appear in different cultures. Sometimes it will change over time. Regardless whether there are one or many versions, the important thing is to make a story your own. I've noticed in myself a tendency to assume I know a story simply because I've read or heard what someone else says about it. Whenever I've gone back to the original material, I've been surprised. If you look through sources of tales, you'll soon find a story that sticks with you, that seems to contain a secret. That's the one to tell in a group. When I've taken the trouble to learn a story and share it, it doesn't leave me. The experience has been more powerful than simply reading.

Jacob and Wilhelm Grimm were the pioneer German scholars who sought out storytellers and copied down their tales without embellishment. They first published them in 1812. Ralph Manheim's *Grimms' Tales for Young and Old* (Anchor Press/Doubleday) is an excellent translation of the Grimm Brothers' work. Iona and Peter Opie's *The Classic Fairy Tales* (Oxford University Press) gives the earliest surviving printed text for twenty-four tales; it's a fascinating introduction to how stories are collected. Other good sources of stories are *American Indian Myths and Legends* (Erdoes and Ortiz, Pantheon Books), *Seven Arrows* (Hyemeyohsts Storm, Ballentine Books), *Italian Folktales* (Italo Calvino, Pantheon Books), *Russian Fairy Tales* (Aleksandor Afanas'ev, Pantheon Books), *World Tales* (Idries Shah, Harcourt Brace Jovanovich). Pantheon publishes a fine library of fairy tales and folklore, including collections of Chinese, Japanese, British, American, French, Arab, African, Irish, Norwegian and Yiddish tales.

The Mabinogion (Jeffrey Gantz, Penguin; also, Lady Charlotte Guest's 1849 version, the first English translation, is available through LIMBUS—see under "Catalogues" below) is the great medieval collection of Welsh myths, which includes stories of Arthur. There isn't a definitive version of the Arthurian legend; succeeding ages have re-shaped it in their own ways. *The Arthurian Legends, An Illustrated Anthology* (Richard Barber, Dorset Press) gives a good overview. Malory's *Le Morte D'Arthur* (Janet Cowan's edition of Caxton's 1485 text, Penguin) itself is a synthesis of earlier medieval narratives. Penguin also publishes, with a glossary, the Middle English text of *Sir Gawain and the Green Knight*. Joseph Bedier provides an elegant retelling of *Tristan and Iseult* (Vintage Books). Wolfram Von Eschenbach's *Parzival* (Helen Mustard and Charles Passage, Vintage), written around 1200, is a celebrated account of the grail myth.

Gods and Heroes—Myths and Epics of Ancient Greece (Gustav Schwab, Pantheon) is a good source of Greek stories, as is Robert Graves' *The Greek Myths* (Penguin Books). Robert Fitzgerald has done beautiful translations of *The Iliad* and *The Odyssey* (Anchor Books, Doubleday). Each religion and culture has its own ancient repository of myths and stories—*The Mahabarata* in Hinduism, *The Bible* in Judaism and Christianity, etc.

Out of these many collections, a few stories have stood out for me personally: "The Wedding of Sir Gawain and Dame Ragnell" (narrated in *Bullfinch's Mythology*, Modern Library); "One Man-Two Man", Robert Johnson's cassette of this American Indian tale (Tape No. 8200X) is available for $9 from the San Diego Friends of Jung Center (3525 Front St., San Diego, 92103, (619-291-0384); from Grimms' (story number in parenthesis), "The Frog King" (1), "Faithful John" (6), "The Girl Without Hands (Silver Hands)" (31), "The Six Swans" (49), "Allerleirauh (Thousandfurs)" (65), "The Gnome" (91), "The Devil's Grimy Brother" (100), "Bearskin" (101), "The Two Traveling Companions" (107), "Hans My Hedgehog" (108), "Iron Hans" (136), "The Drummer" (193), "Old Rinkrank" (196), "King Thrushbeard" (52), "The Boy Who Left Home to Find Out About the Shivers (Fear)" (4); from the Pantheon *Russian Fairy Tales*, "The Maiden Tsar", "Maria Morevna", "The Firebird and Princess Vasilisa", "The Sea King and Vasilisa the Wise"; from *The Mabinogion*, "Pwyll Lord of Dyved", "Owein, or The Countess of the Fountain". The National Association for the Preservation and Perpetuation of Storytelling (NAPPS, P.O. Box 309, Jonesborough, TN 37659, 800-525-4514) keeps track of story-telling festivals, workshops and performances throughout the country.

Interpretations of Myths and Fairy Tales

What makes interpretative work on stories valuable is not so much learning what an author concludes, but following his or her thinking process. The writers who illuminate the reciprocity between life and stories go back and forth between the personal and universal, the psychological and the mythological. Reading some books here, I began to see that many dilemmas I faced were not the physical or psychological problems I had supposed, but problems which could be solved only on the level of the imagination.

Joseph Campbell articulates what it is to think mythologically. Some of his work is available through Ally Press and LIMBUS (see under "Catalogues") but his books are now in most bookstores as well. Even if you've seen the six-hour *Power of Myth* interviews with Bill Moyers on PBS, read the book of the same title (Doubleday), which is not a transcript but a complement to the series. *The Hero With a Thousand Faces* (Princeton University Press), his first book, is also an inspiring place to begin.

Robert Johnson is an analytical psychologist and teacher. He has the gift of taking complex ideas and expressing them in simple language, and he writes movingly about the interplay of mythology and personality. In *He* (Perennial Library), *She* (Perennial Library) and *We* (HarperCollins), he uses myths to demonstrate the development of men, women and romantic relationships. Reading these books (*He* is a personal favorite) gives a clear idea of the power of relating stories to life.

In his conferences, interviews, performances and workshops over the past decade, Robert Bly has begun to apply mythological thinking to the problems of men, leading them literally back into the forest onto sacred ground. His reflections were first published in an interview by Keith Thompson ("What Men Really Want," *New Age Magazine*) in 1982. When I attended my first men's conference, I met men who, knowing nothing about Bly, had crossed the country to be there because of that interview. In the atmosphere of the conferences, ideas sprouted like wildflowers. Two subsequent monographs (*The Pillow and the Key* and *When a Hair Turns Gold*, Ally Press) expanded Bly's thinking. In 1990, he incorporated these and other material into *Iron John* (Addison-Wesley), his extended commentary on the Grimm's tale.

The strong body of interpretative writing by Jung's great pupil, Marie-Louise von Franz includes: *Interpretation of Fairytales, Problems of the Feminine in Fairytales, Shadow and Evil in Fairytales* (all published by Spring), *Individuation in Fairy Tales* (Shambala). Von Franz has also written a landmark study in male psychology, *Puer Aeternus* (The Eternal Boy) (Sigo Publications).

The psychologist James Hillman (proprietor of Spring Press) frequently co-leads men's conferences with Bly and Michael Meade. His collection of essays, *Puer Papers* (Spring), is a response to Von Franz's ideas on the Puer. His many other books are in the Spring catalogue. Especially recommended are *The Dream and the Underworld*, *Archetypal Psychology*, *Loose Ends* and *Healing Fiction*. Robert Moore, another teacher at the conferences, has done a superb series of audio tapes (available from LIMBUS and Ally Press) on the masculine figures of the king, the warrior, the magician and the lover. He and Douglas Gillette have incorporated this material into their book *King, Warrior, Magician, Lover* (HarperCollins). You also might want to look at *The Ravaged Bridegroom* (Inner City Books) by psychologist Marion Woodman.

Writing on mythological motifs dovetails with ritual and ethnographic studies. The LIMBUS and Spring catalogues below offer scholarly inquiries such as by Campbell's teacher Heinrich Zimmer (*The King and the Corpse*, Princeton University Press), John Layard (*A Celtic Quest*, Spring Publications), Joseph Henderson (*Thresholds of Initiation*, Wesleyan University Press) and others. In *Betwixt and Between* (Open Court) Louise Mahdi has gathered a group of compelling essays on masculine and feminine initiation. In 1980, an exhibition called *The Wildman: Medieval Myth and Symbolism* was presented at the Cloisters in New York City. The catalogue (Timothy Husband, Metropolitan Museum of Art) details the appearance of the Wildman in Europe in the Middle Ages, and contains many powerful images.

Inner Work

Though the ritual group focuses on men collectively, I want to say something about the work men do on their own. Some years ago I had a recurring dream that terrorists were pursuing me; they wanted to get their hands on some sacred scrolls I was charged with protecting. I think of inner work (Robert Johnson's term) as learning to read the writing on your own sacred scrolls. I've tried to do my "learning how to learn" outside ritual groups, not in them. For me, a good therapist has been an important avenue; and a good therapist was someone who gave me insight and support to make meaningful changes in my life.

Of the inner work one can do, dream work may be the most valuable. Ann Faraday's *The Dream Game* (Perennial Library) is a useful, down-to-earth book on interpreting your dreams. Marie-Louise von Franz has done a wonderful cycle of twenty half-hour films, *The Way of the Dream*, presented by many local Jung societies a few years ago, which I hope will someday find its way onto public television. She was asked questions on a series of dreams, and seemed to answer with the voice of the Oracle. Windrose Films has published the transcript of the interviews.

Robert Johnson's *Inner Work* (HarperCollins) is an important book on dreams which goes beyond interpretation. He believes it is essential not only to take unconscious material into consciousness, but from consciousness into action in the world. He presents an approach to dreams that shows how to incorporate them into rituals. This book is useful for men who want some practical guidance on how to create meaningful rituals, both for themselves and in groups.

I'll include a few other books in this genre known to generate extensive heat in groups. Alice Miller's *The Drama of the Gifted Child* (formerly *Prisoners of Childhood*, Basic Books) incised and cauterized wounds that had gone untended in me for years. Both Gershen Kaufman's *Shame* (Schenkman Books) and Robert Stein's *Incest and Human Love* (Spring) worked similarly in some close friends. *A Little Book on the Human Shadow* (HarperCollins) is Bly's personal and poetic rumination on shadow and projection. Working on projections is important and difficult. Chapter seven in Ken Wilbur's *No Boundary* (Whole Mind Series, Center Publications) and Marie-Louise von Franz's *Projection and Re-Collection in Jungian Psychology* (Open Court) are both very helpful. The first eighty pages of M. Scott Peck's *The Road Less Travelled* (Touchstone) present an original and invaluable discussion of discipline. Bernie Zilbergeld's point of view in *Male Sexuality* (Bantam Books) promotes a healthy re-examination of some male stereotypes.

Poetry and Essays

Recognizing or re-recognizing a poet who speaks in the language of your heart is a joyful discovery. One clue: when you first encounter a poem, read it aloud and pretend someone is reading to you. When you find a good one memorize it. Someday you'll be moved to give it to a group and it will be yours to give. It's a memorable evening when one man after another rises to offer a poem.

Robert Bly has translated numerous poets from other cultures whose poems awaken the spirit. Many mentioned here can be found in the Ally Press Catalogue. Bly has done versions (renderings of another's translation) of three ecstatic poets of medieval India and Persia: Kabir (*The Kabir Book*, Beacon Press), six poems of Mirabai (*Mirabai*, Red Ozier Press), and Rumi (*When Grapes Turn to Wine* and with Coleman Barks, *Night and Sleep*, both Yellow Moon Press.) He's also translated Antonio Machado (*Times Alone*, Wesleyan Press), Juan Ramon Jiminez, Pablo Neruda, Cesar Vallejo, Tomas Transtromer and Francis Ponge. He and Stephen Mitchell have each done fine volumes of Rainer Maria Rilke. Get them both. You can find a good cross-section of Bly's own poetry in his *Selected Poems* (HarperCollins). *News of the Universe* (Sierra Club) is his marvelous anthology of "poems of twofold consciousness."

A few other poets who stir deep feelings in their readers and listeners are: Wallace Stevens, Anna Akhmatova, Czeslaw Milosz, Robert Hass, Carolyn Forche, Margaret Atwood, W.B. Yeats, D.H. Lawrence, Gary Snyder, Etheridge Knight, Louis Jenkins, Elizabeth Bishop, Nikki Giovanni, Marianne Moore, William Carlos Williams, William Stafford, Basho. Lao Tse's *Tao Te Ching* (The Way of Life) is a book I like to keep at my bedside. I also want to mention Galway Kinnell's poem "The Bear" and *Lyrics of the Troubadours and Trouveres* (Frederick Goldin, Peter Smith Publishers), a collection of the Provencal poets.

Perceptive criticism can illuminate poetry. *Singular Voices* (Stephen Berg, Avon), *Goatfoot Milktongue Twinbird* (Donald Hall, University of Michigan Press), *Twentieth Century Pleasures* (Robert Hass, Ecco Press) contain essays which bring the meaning of poems closer. *Poets and Writers* (72 Spring St., New York, NY 10012) is a well written magazine containing insightful interviews and articles on poetry and writing in general.

Some literary essays and letters reach an extraordinary level of feeling, such as Rilke's *Letters to a Young Poet* (M.D. Herter Norton, W.W. Norton) and *Rilke On Love and Other Difficulties* (John Mood, W.W. Norton). Kafka's astonishing letters to his father are in *The Basic Kafka* (Eric Heller, Pocket Books). *Dear Theo* contains Vincent Van Gogh's letters to his brother (Irving Stone, Signet). D.H. Lawrence's *Fantasia of the Unconscious* and *Psychoanalysis and the Unconscious* have been published in one volume by Penguin. Virginia Woolf's *A Room of One's Own* (Harcourt Brace Jovanovich) helps to measure the psychic forces aligned against the feminine, and the importance of a container for creative work. The writing of Northrop Frye clarifies the interaction between literature and myth. *Northrop Frye On Culture and Literature* (Robert Denham, University of Chicago Press) and *The Secular*

Scripture (Harvard University Press) are two very accessible works. Also, I want to suggest Michael Ventura's *Shadow Dancing in the USA* (Jeremy Tarcher), a collection of essays from his *L.A. Weekly* column.

Literature, Movies and Music

Our culture contains many diversions that are banal, disheartening or empty of spirit, and which distract us from relating to one another from the depth of ourselves. Yet there is also literature and art which supports us in gathering together, learning together, feeling together. I want to list some books, films and music which in some way confirm that what the ritual groups are trying to do is right, and that ritual and mythology give essential direction to the development of manhood.

T. H. White's *The Once and Future King* (G.P. Putnam and Sons) describes the education of the young Arthur by Merlin. *A River Runs Through It* (University of Chicago) is Norman Maclean's account of fly fishing in Idaho with his brother. Ursula Le Guin's *The Earthsea Trilogy* (Parnassus [Part I], Atheneum [Parts II and III]) is a striking tale of initiation and shadow. Marion Zimmer Bradley's *The Mists of Avalon* (Ballentine Books) retells the Arthurian legend from a feminine point of view. In *The King Must Die* (Bantam) Mary Renault recreates the ancient Greek myth of Theseus.

D. M. Thomas' *The White Hotel* (Viking Press) amazes with its conception of the psyche, somewhat as Peter Birkhauser's paintings do. James Hilton's *Lost Horizon* (Pocket Books) encapsulates how the mind seduces with images of perfection. *Mr. Bridge* (Evan S. Connell, North Point Press) is a cautionary portrait of a withered male psyche. Isaac Bashevis Singer and Gabriel Garcia Marquez write stories of inspiring soulfulness.

Four heroes of mine are men who write eloquently on the spirit of the natural world. Gary Snyder (*The Practice of the Wild*, North Point Press), Peter Matthiessen (*The Snow Leopard*, Penguin Books), Wendell Berry (*Collected Poems*, North Point Press), Aldo Leopold (*The River of the Mother of God*, University of Wisconsin Press) have spent their lives listening to the land; they have given time and energy to preserve and protect it. This husbanding, grandfathering work is a mark of developed men.

I would like to add some books of fiction and memoir recommended by men in my group: about Africa, *Lightning Bird* (Lyall Watson, Touchstone) and *A Story Like the Wind* (Lawrence Van der Post, Harcourt Brace Jovanovitch); about Australia, *The Song Lines* (Bruce

Chatwin, Penguin); about inner work, *The Words to Say It* (Marie Cardinal, VanVactor & Goodheart); about failure, *Act One* (Moss Hart, Random House).

Picking out movies seems completely subjective, but I know a number that have affected both myself and other men. Ken Burns' recent PBS series, *The Civil War*, is very poignant and I strongly recommend seeing it for a perception of how war affects men's lives, and how this particular war affected this country. *Glory* is similarly moving. These are some resonant films of boyhood and adolescence: *The Stone Boy, Runaway Train, My Life as a Dog, Fanny and Alexander, The Emerald Forest, Hope and Glory, Diner, Third Man on the Mountain* (a favorite from my childhood, produced by Disney), *Taps, The Great Santini, Stand By Me*. The next three films take art near the realm of myth: *Excalibur* (the first half, anyway), *The Man Who Would Be King* and maybe (but probably not, though I love it still) *Robin and Marian*. *Zorba the Greek* is about a real Wildman, *Fatal Attraction* a modern imagining of a fairy tale witch, *Brazil* a nightmare about the consequences of denying the psyche. *The Collector* is about confusing the inner woman with the outer, *Deliverance* , the violence of undeveloped males, and *Witness*, the unity underlying apparent opposites.

A word about music. One reason I like *Shadow Dancing* is an essay "Hear That Long Snake Moan," in which Ventura explains how the rock music he loves contributes to who he is. There is enormous male strength in Beethoven, Mahler and Stravinsky, and a tenderness in traditional folk music and ballads that grounds the listener in the earth. The Lost Dogs went one night to hear the Chieftains, a traditional Irish group, and I also remember a meeting we spent transfixed by a tape of hundreds of Sufis chanting in Konya. Music sometimes takes you where words can't; if you've played an instrument for ten years, or have loved Dylan or Paul Horn or Muddy Waters as long as you can remember, then give these to other men with all the reverence you can.

In *Drumming At the Edge of Magic* (Mickey Hart with Jay Stevens, Harper San Francisco) Grateful Dead drummer Mickey Hart describes his lifelong exploration of the intangible energy of drums. The bibliography includes a list of recordings of rhythms from many cultures. Many men in groups either purchase or make their own drums, and a variety of percussion instruments from native cultures over the world are now crafted in this country. When you see a man playing a drum you like, ask him where he got it. Some of the periodicals below contain advertisements concerning drums, drumming and dancing. You might contact B.D. Drums for their catalog (PO Box

2117, Vashon, WA 98070, 800-767-6120) or drummaker N. Aidoo Holmes (633 Allison St. NW, Washington, DC 26011, 202-882-4649). The Sounds True Catalogue (1825 Pearl St., Dept W91, Boulder, CO 80302, 800-333-9185, ext. 275) markets a cassette on how to play traditional African and Latin rhythms.

Catalogues and Presses, Periodicals, Men's Studies, Conferences, Miscellany

The sense of community among men is growing and more is being offered to men than ever before. In a recent interview in the *L.A. Times*, Robert Bly identified seven different "men's movements." As you browse through publications, articles, advertising, etc., you'll see a range of choices. I've listed here those things that I'm aware of which are consistent with my own commitment to the ritual group.

Some **catalogues and presses** are sources of books and recordings for ritual groups. The people behind these noted below have a respect for the psyche and the slow, serious nature of the work:

Ally Press Center (524 Orleans St., St. Paul, MN 55107, 800-729-3002) is both a distributing and publishing house. It originally formed in 1986 to gather all the publications of Robert Bly in one catalogue. Their list has expanded to include books and/or cassettes by James Hillman, Michael Meade, Robert Moore, Joseph Campbell and others. They have begun publishing new material of interest to men (including the present work) and a quarterly newsletter, *Dragonsmoke*, which contains a speaking/teaching schedule for Bly, Hillman, Meade and Moore. Joining their bookclub ($15 initiation fee, $5 yearly renewal) qualifies members for a 15% discount, subscription to *Dragonsmoke*, and first class mailings of schedule and catalog updates. Many works I mention here are available through them. Write or call for their free catalogue.

LIMBUS (P.O. Box 364, Vashon, WA 98070, 800-233-6984) is Michael Meade's organization. Their catalogue is free and includes books and cassettes by Meade, Bly, Hillman and Moore, and a selection of works on mythology, ritual and initiation. Meade is a drummer, storyteller and lover of mythology. He began leading conferences with Bly in 1984, and has been an important force behind men's gatherings in North America. He's introduced drumming to the conferences and has popularized many stories .

Spring Publications (P.O. Box 222069, Dallas, TX 75222, 214-943-4093) is James Hillman's press. Their catalogue is analytical (Jungian) in orientation and includes many worthwhile books, some of which I've mentioned here. They've performed a service in reissuing some important titles which were out of print. Write to be included in their mailings.

Oral Tradition Archives (1104 Lincoln Ave., Pacific Grove, CA 93950, 408-373-1110) tapes various events for men. For reasons of confidentiality, many of their cassettes are available only to participants. But they also edit and release some sets to the public. They do their work with integrity. I particularly recommend *Men and the Life of Desire*, a recording of a "day for men" with Bly, Meade and Hillman in San Francisco. Their tapes are available through both LIMBUS and Ally Press, or you can order direct. Call or write for a list.

Recent years have seen a flurry of **periodicals** of interest to men. The style, often a mixture of poetry, reflection, story and reportage, was set by *The Men's Journal* (Woodacre, CA, Yevrah Ornstein, ed.), now defunct. Back issues of *The Men's Journal* are available from another quarterly, *Wingspan* (P.O. Box 1491, Manchester-by-the-Sea, MA 01944), which prints interviews, a calendar and list of resources for men.

Inroads (P.O. Box 14944 University Station, Minneapolis, MN 55414) publishes some thoughtful articles by, for, and about men, as does *JOURNEYMEN* (513 Chester Turnpike, Candia, NH 03034). *MAN!* (1611 West Sixth St., Austin, TX 78703) is another effort in this direction, though primarily psychological. The following three, not specifically for men, contain writing that is often inspiriting: *The Sun* (107 North Roberson St., Chapel Hill, NC 27516), a highly reflective magazine (which interviewed Michael Meade in April, 1989 and James Hillman in April, 1991); *Common Boundary* (7005 Florida St, Chevy Chase, MD 20815), which characterizes itself as "between spirituality and psychotherapy," is consistently rewarding; *Parabola* (565 Broadway, New York, NY 10012), a journal exploring mythology and spirituality, is occasionally worthwhile.

The field of **men's studies** is a relatively new academic discipline. I'd like to specify a few of the books used in some courses, which, though not about ritual or mythology, touch on themes of interest to ritual groups: *The Myth of Masculinity* (Joe Pleck, M.I.T. Press), *A Choice of Heroes* (Mark Gerzon, Houghton Mifflin Company), *Men and Friendship* (Stuart Miller, HM Press), *Finding Our Fathers* (Samuel Osherson, The Free Press), *About Men* (Edward Klein and Don Erickson, Pocket Books), *In a Different Voice* (Carol Gilligan, Harvard University Press).

A men's **conference** adds dimension to the work in ritual groups. It increases the drama, contains surprise, and forces the individual to stretch. If you haven't been to one, go. It's worth the time and expense. In my experience, a week with a hundred men is a more profound experience than a weekend with three hundred or a day with five hundred. Generally these events are organized by individuals or small groups of men. You can find a listing in *Dragonsmoke* or *Wingspan*. Since conferences fill quickly it's important to send in a deposit as soon as you can. The one I'm most familiar with takes place in Mendocino each summer and has its own mailing list for flyers. To receive one, send a note to Martin Keogh (c/o The Dancing Ground, P.O. Box 2645, Berkeley, CA 94702). The leaders I know best are Bly, Meade, Hillman, Moore and tracker John Stokes; they work around the country annually.

A miscellaneous note: It can be awkward to sit without lumbar support. B.J. Industries (P.O. Box 27, Phoenix, MD 21131) manufactures the "backjack" chair, a one-piece, stackable, floor-sitting backrest. It's sturdy, comfortable, unobtrusive and just right for groups meeting in a workroom or garage. Call (301) 771-0050 or order by mail; worth the $27 price.

Wayne Liebman (kneeling, second from left)
is a physician practicing in Los Angeles. In January, 1984 he
organized a week long men's conference with Robert Bly and
Michael Meade which stimulated the creation of a small ritual
men's group, the Lost Dog Men's Council. He is currently writing a novel about medicine and dreaming.

The graphic device on the cover is a talisman called "Uenukut," or "God Symbol," and was used by the ancient Maori people to focus on a superhuman life-giving force. Standing 8 feet, 8 inches high, it was rediscovered in 1906 in New Zealand's Lake Ngaroto.